MOSASAURS

BY KATE MOENING
ILLUSTRATIONS BY MAT EDWARDS

EPIC

BELLWETHER MEDIA • MINNEAPOLIS, MN

EPIC BOOKS are no ordinary books. They burst with intense action, high-speed heroics, and shadows of the unknown. Are you ready for an Epic adventure?

This edition first published in 2023 by Bellwether Media, Inc.

No part of this publication may be reproduced in whole or in part without written permission of the publisher. For information regarding permission, write to Bellwether Media, Inc., Attention: Permissions Department, 6012 Blue Circle Drive, Minnetonka, MN 55343.

Library of Congress Cataloging-in-Publication Data

LC record for Mosasaurs available at: https://lccn.loc.gov/2022050376

Text copyright © 2023 by Bellwether Media, Inc. EPIC and associated logos are trademarks and/or registered trademarks of Bellwether Media, Inc.

Editor: Betsy Rathburn   Designer: Jeffrey Kollock

Printed in the United States of America, North Mankato, MN.

TABLE OF CONTENTS

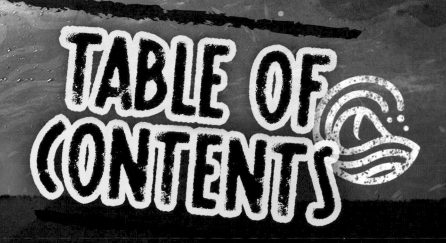

WHAT WERE MOSASAURS?

PRONUNCIATION

MOH-zuh-SORE

Mosasaurs were huge ocean **reptiles**. They first appeared about 100 million years ago.

MAP OF THE WORLD

Late Cretaceous period

Mosasaurs lived during the Late **Cretaceous period**. This was at the end of the **Mesozoic era**.

6

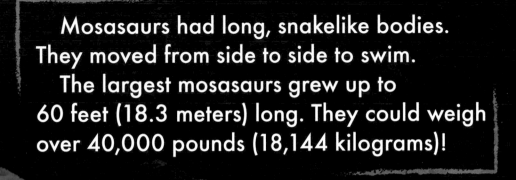

Mosasaurs had long, snakelike bodies.
They moved from side to side to swim.
The largest mosasaurs grew up to
60 feet (18.3 meters) long. They could weigh
over 40,000 pounds (18,144 kilograms)!

SIZE COMPARISON

about as long as a semi-truck trailer

Long tails pushed mosasaurs through water.
They steered with paddle-shaped fins.

fins

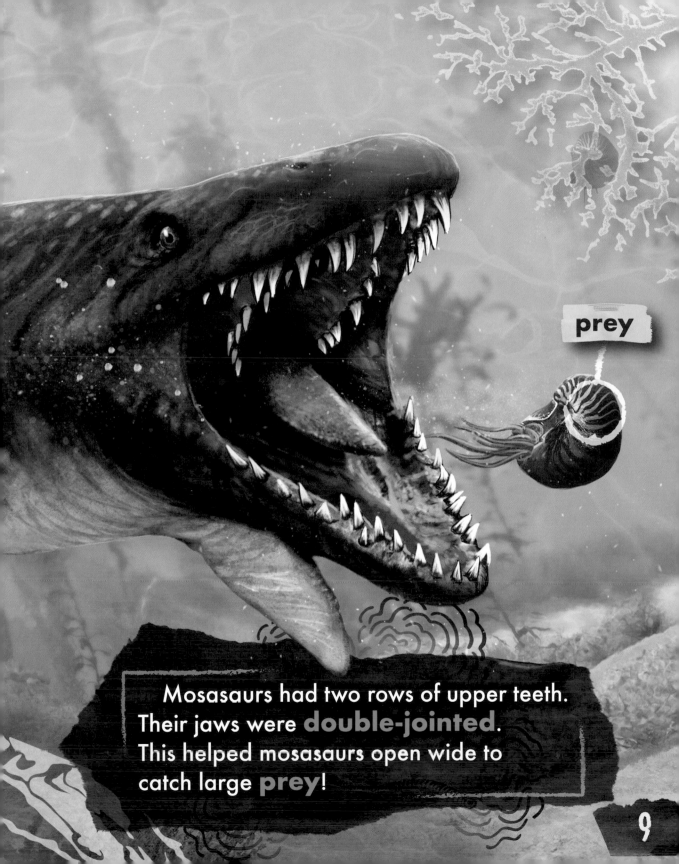

prey

Mosasaurs had two rows of upper teeth. Their jaws were **double-jointed**. This helped mosasaurs open wide to catch large **prey**!

THE LIVES OF MOSASAURS

SHELL EATERS

Some mosasaurs ate crabs and clams. These mosasaurs had mushroom-shaped teeth! Their teeth were good for breaking hard shells.

Mosasaurs were **carnivores**. They ate fish, squids, turtles, and even other mosasaurs!

Mosasaurs were usually slow swimmers. But they could swim fast for short periods of time. They sped up to catch food!

MOSASAUR DIET

squids

turtles

mosasaurs

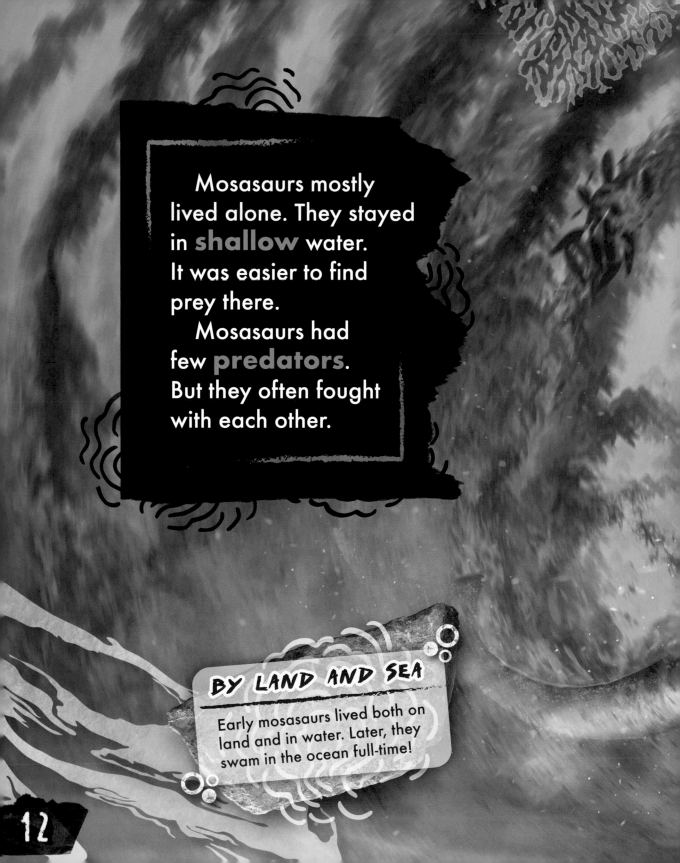

Mosasaurs mostly lived alone. They stayed in **shallow** water. It was easier to find prey there.

Mosasaurs had few **predators**. But they often fought with each other.

BY LAND AND SEA

Early mosasaurs lived both on land and in water. Later, they swam in the ocean full-time!

13

Mosasaurs gave birth to live young. The babies were easy prey to other mosasaurs and sharks.

Female mosasaurs may have lived in groups to protect their young.

FOSSILS AND EXTINCTION

asteroid

Mosasaurs went **extinct** at the end of the Cretaceous period. A huge **asteroid** caused changes to Earth's **climate**.

Mosasaurs could not survive these changes.

The first mosasaur **fossil** was found in the 1760s. It was discovered in a mine in the Netherlands.

FREQUENT FINDS

At the end of the Mesozoic era, mosasaurs were the most common ocean reptiles. Scientists are still finding their fossils all over the world!

fossil

FIRST MOSASAUR FOSSIL FOUND

mosasaur fossil

EUROPE

FOUND in the **1760s**

LOCATED Maastricht, the Netherlands

Mosasaur fossils have been found on every **continent**. These powerful reptiles ruled the ancient seas!

GET TO KNOW THE MOSASAUR

WEIGHT
over 40,000 pounds
(18,144 kilograms)

long tail

FOOD

squids

mosasaurs

turtles

SIZE up to 60 feet (18.3 meters) long

Paleozoic | Mesozoic | Cretaceous | Cenozoic

two rows of upper teeth

double-jointed jaws

FIRST FOSSIL COLLECTED

in the 1760s by Jean Baptiste Drouin

LOCATION

oceans around the world

GLOSSARY

asteroid—a rocky object in space that travels around planets or stars

carnivores—animals that only eat meat

climate—the long-term weather in a particular place

continent—one of Earth's seven large land masses

Cretaceous period—the last period of the Mesozoic era that occurred between 145 million and 66 million years ago; the Late Cretaceous period began around 100 million years ago.

double-jointed—having a joint that lets body parts move in more than one direction

extinct—no longer living

fossil—the remains of a living thing that lived long ago

Mesozoic era—a time in history that happened about 252 million to 66 million years ago; the first birds, mammals, and flowering plants appeared on Earth during the Mesozoic era.

predators—animals that hunt other animals for food

prey—animals that are hunted by other animals for food

reptiles—cold-blooded animals that have backbones and lay eggs

shallow—not deep

TO LEARN MORE

AT THE LIBRARY

Hansen, Grace. *Mosasaurus*. Minneapolis, Minn.: Abdo, 2021.

Taylor, Charlotte. *Digging Up Sea Creature Fossils*. New York, N.Y.: Enslow Publishing, 2022.

Yang, Yang. *The Secrets of Ancient Sea Monsters: PNSO Encyclopedia for Children*. Dallas, Tex.: Brown Books Kids, 2021.

ON THE WEB

FACTSURFER

Factsurfer.com gives you a safe, fun way to find more information.

1. Go to www.factsurfer.com.

2. Enter "mosasaurs" into the search box and click 🔍 .

3. Select your book cover to see a list of related content.

INDEX

The images in this book are reproduced through the courtesy of: Mat Edwards, front cover, pp. 1, 2, 3, 4-5, 6-7, 8-9, 10-11, 12-13, 14-15, 16-17, 18-19, 20-21; Ghedoghedo/ Wikipedia, p. 19 (fossil).